AF261455

The Adventures of Peter the Park Bench

By: Nedia Lee

Hi, I am Peter, the Park Bench.
Come join me for a beautiful day in the park.
Who will we see? What will we see? I am not sure,
but I know we will see new things that we can share with our family and friend

Let us begin our journey to the park.

The first things I notice as we walk into the park are the tall,
beautiful trees with all types of leaves
that are different colors, shapes and sizes.
There are red leaves and green leaves.
There are also yellow leaves and orange leaves.
There are even leaves that seem to look like rainbows.

When our friendly sun shines through the trees and the wind begins to blow,
the leaves seem to come alive.
They are smiling and dancing as they glide through the air.
They go left and right and backwards and forwards
as they slowly fall to the ground.

When the leaves finally land,
they paint the ground with an array of colors.
The leaves only add to the beautiful park landscape
which has many flowers of different colors,
shapes and sizes. Can you see all the beautiful flowers?

There are red flowers and white flowers.
There are also yellow flowers and orange flowers.
There are even flowers that seem to look like rainbows.
These flowers enjoy each other's company.
They need the sun and the rain to grow and stay healthy.

Look! Look! What do you see?

I see a squirrel. No, I see two….three…..four squirrels.

They are having so much fun running and playing.
One of them sits on a branch eating an acorn,
the other is clinging on to the tree trunk watching the other two
playing in the leaves that have fallen to the ground.
I wonder if they are a family. What do you think?

Oh my, a little red bird has landed on my bench.
It is singing a song and calling more of his friends.
Chirp...Chirp...Chirp...Chirp....

There comes a yellow bird and orange bird.
More birds begin to drop by for a visit…..a blue bird and green bird.
Other birds that seem to look like rainbows also join us.
They all begin to sing……..Chirp……Chirp……Chirp…….Chirp.

The birds begin to slowly fly up...up....up......to the sky.
I don't know why because we were having so much fun.
Bye, bye little birds.
Thank you for being my friends and spending some time with me.

What is that I hear? The sound is getting louder and louder.
Woof......Woof......Woof......

Oh no, dogs of different breeds are heading towards my bench.
They are different colors and sizes.
They even have different hair and fur.
Some dogs are big and some dogs are small.
There are even some dogs
wearing clothes that
have the colors of the rainbow.

I see black dogs and brown dogs. I also see white dogs and dogs with spots.
Some of them have long hair and fur and others have short hair and fur.
They love playing around me. They are playing on me and under me.
They are playing behind me and in front of me.

I wonder what would happen if I throw this orange ball.

Look at the dogs run. They all want to play with the ball.
The ball is bouncing and bouncing.
The dogs are jumping up and down and running all around.
They are enjoying the bouncing ball.

The ball has rolled under a tree. One of the dogs has placed his paw on it.
I guess he is waiting for someone to throw it again.
The rest of the dogs have started to run away.

Wait, I see someone.

It is a little boy.

He picks up the ball and starts to play with this dog.
I guess this little boy is his owner.
I am so glad to see them playing together.

I see more children joining in on the fun. They all are playing together.
They keep bouncing and tossing the ball to each other
and running back and forth.
They are throwing the ball into a basket.
The basket is up high. Can you guess the name of the game?

You are right! They are playing basketball.

The children are all different. Some are taller than others.
Some are girls and some are boys.
Some have long hair and some have short hair.
Some have black hair and some have brown hair.
Some even have yellow hair and others have red hair.
They are wearing different types of clothes and different types of shoes and
their socks are the colors of the rainbow.

They are all friends.

I think it is getting late because the children begin to leave.
They stop playing and let the ball bounce into a bush.
When the ball hits the bush, butterflies begin flying away.

I see red butterflies and yellow butterflies.
I also see orange butterflies and blue butterflies.
There are even butterflies that have the colors of the rainbow.
They are flying all around me. I think they are trying to find a place to rest.

Look at how beautiful they are. Would you like to follow them?

They are flying towards the flowers.
They are trying to find shelter under the leaves.
Let us take a closer look. I wonder what else we will find.

I see a ladybug. Do you see the ladybug?

I see a caterpillar. Do you see the caterpillar?

I see an ant. Do you see the ant?

I see a spider. Do you see the spider?

I see a beetle. Do you see the beetle?

I see a grasshopper. Do you see the grasshopper?

There are many things to see if you go to the park.
Remember not to go alone and never talk to strangers.
You need to go with a friend or go with your mom or dad.

I hope you liked our adventure in the park.
If you are looking for another adventure, look for my friend Zoe.
She is Zoe the Zoo Bench.
She will take you on a wild adventure through the zoo.

Bye, bye…….